LOCAL RED

HASTINGS
BEXHILL

CONTENTS

Page Layout & Road Map   2
2½ Miles to 1 Inch

Hastings Enlarged Centre   3
7 Inches to 1 Mile

Street Maps   4-20
4 Inches to 1 Mile

Index to Streets   21

Redbooks showing the way

Every effort has been made to verify the accuracy of information in this book but the publishers cannot accept responsibility for expense or loss caused by an error or omission.

Information that will be of assistance to the user of the maps will be welcomed.

The representation on these maps of a road, track or path is no evidence of the existence of a right of way.

Street plans prepared and published by ESTATE PUBLICATIONS, Bridewell House, TENTERDEN, KENT. The Publishers acknowledge the co-operation of the local authorities of towns represented in this atlas.

Ordnance Survey This product includes mapping data licensed from Ordnance Survey® with the permission of the Controller of Her Majesty's Stationery Office.

www.ESTATE-PUBLICATIONS.co.uk

Printed by Ajanta Offset, New Delhi, India.

LEGEND

- ▰ Motorway
- ▰ 'A' Road
- ▰ 'B' Road
- Minor Road
- Pedestrianised / Restricted Access
- Track
- Built Up Area
- Footpath
- Stream
- River
- Lock Canal
- Railway / Station
- ● Post Office
- P P+ Car Park / Park & Ride
- C Public Convenience
- ✚ Place of Worship
- → One-way Street
- i Tourist Information Centre
- ▲ ▲ Adjoining Pages
- Area Depicting Enlarged Centre
- Emergency Services
- Industrial Buildings
- Leisure Buildings
- Education Buildings
- Hotels etc.
- Retail Buildings
- General Buildings
- Woodland
- Recreation Ground
- Cemetery

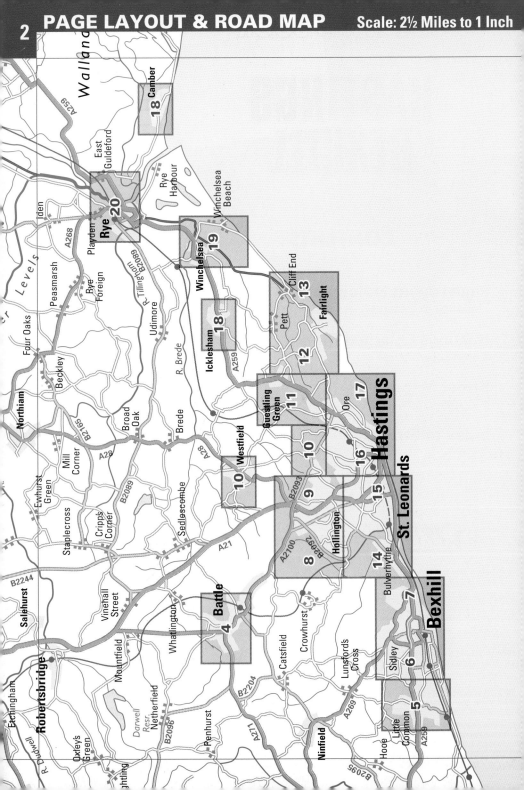

HASTINGS

West Hill

Caves

Recreation Ground

West Hill Cliff Railway

CASTLE (remains of) Arts Centre

Miniature Railway

The Stade

Lifeboat Station

Fishermans Museum

Harbour

Harbour Light

Breakwater

Boating Lake

MARINE PARADE

EAST PARADE

SHOPPING PRECINCT

Castle Rocks

QUEENS RD

ALBERT ROAD

DENMARK PL

HAVELOCK RD

HAROLD PL

CARLISLE PARADE

ROCK

CAMBRIDGE ROAD

BOHEMIA ROAD

PRIORY MEADOW SHOPPING CENTRE

Town Hall

STATION RD

Hastings Station

CAMBRIDGE GDNS

Cornwallis Gardens

Linton Gardens

Museum & Art Gallery

Sports Centre

White Rock Gardens

Falaise Hall

Theatre

Pier

Ambulance Station

Supermarket

WHITE ROCK

EVERSFIELD PL

Subway

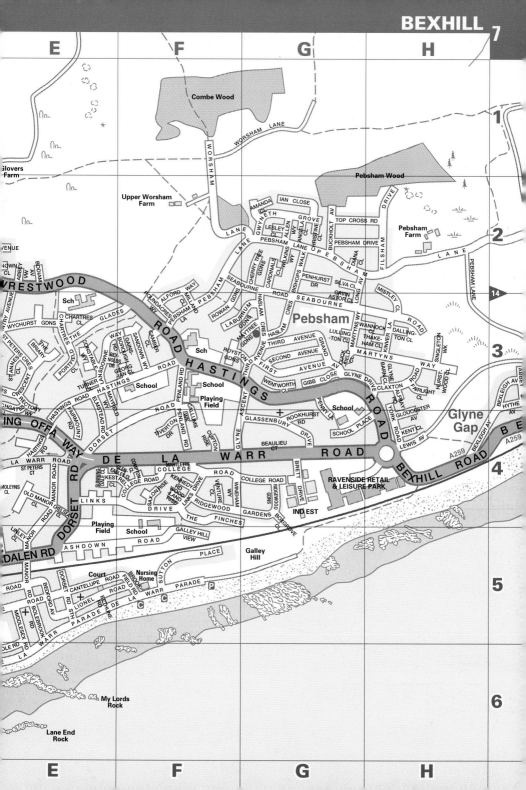

Three Oaks

THREE OAKS

Half House Farm

Fraysland Wood

Church La   Church L

Village Hall

Fraysland Farm

Pound Farm

Eight Acre Wood

Old Coghurst Farm

Hoads Wood

Brickyard Wood

Chapel La Higham Gdns

Coghurst Wood

Hulls Wood

Rock Farm

Guestling Hall Youth Hostel

Ten Acre Wood

Coghurst

Bachelors Bump

Friars Hill   Pett
Road   Pett

Humphreys Farm

Pigeon Cove Shaw

Down Farm

Lidham Farm

Mill Lane   Martineau

Spindlewood Country Holiday Park

School

Mill Farm

Austen Way

Cemy

School

Fire Sta

School

Rec Grnd

Picnic Area

Road   Fairlic

E   F   G   H

Eastlands Shaw

THE GLEBE
ELMS LANE
THE OAK FIELD
PETT ROAD
PETT

Pett

Gatehurst Farm

ROAD PETT

CHICK HILL ROAD

Saxon Shore Way

ROAD PETT LEVEL

1

CANAL BANK

LEVEL

PETT ROAD

PETT ROAD

Old Marsham Farm

Cliff End

X

2

Market Wood

ROAD

CLIFF END LANE

3

PETT LEVEL ROAD

Marsham Farm

Stumblet Wood

ROSEMARY

Wakehams Farm

LANE

PETT LEVEL ROAD

Saxon Shore Way

STREAM LANE

4

Fairlight Cove

BRIAR CL

PRIMROSE HILL

WAITES

SEA ROAD

LEVEL ROAD

ROAD WAY

BROAD WAY

CLINTON WAY

LOWER ROCKMEAD RD

CLIFF WAY

SEA ROAD

5

FAIRLIGHT GDNS

LOWER WAITES LA

THE AVENUE

STOCK DALE

ROCKMEAD ROAD

SHEPHERDS WM

SMUGGLERS

BLACKTHORN WY

SHEPHERDS WAY

BRAMBLE WY

HEATHER WAY

WAY

6

E   F   G   H

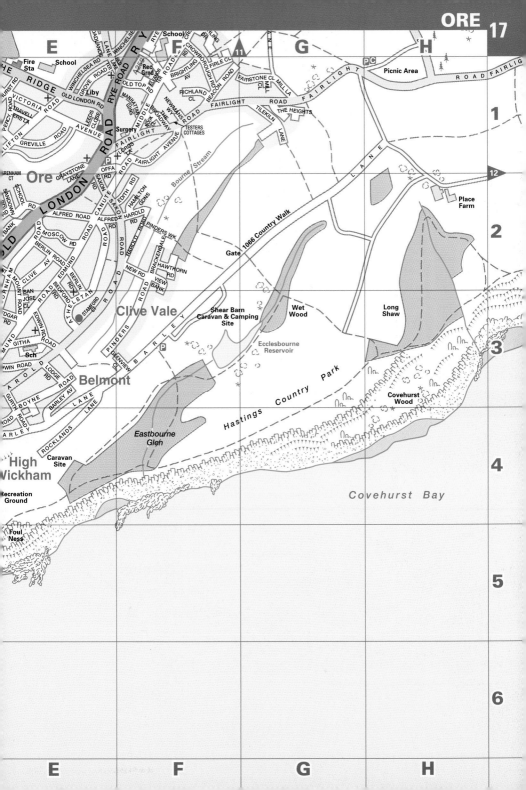

E F 11 G H

Fire Sta School School Cranley

THE RIDGE WINCHELSEA ROAD BROOMGROVE ROAD DADLANDS RYE Rec Grnd BRIGHTLING Picnic Area ROAD FAIRLIG

VICTORIA ROAD Liby Rec Grnd CROMBOROUGH RD FIRLE CL BRIGHTLING AV FAIRSTONE CL MILL LA FAIRLIGHT ROAD

TRAVELL ERS LA OLD LONDON RD OLD TOP RD RYE RICHLAND CL FIRLE CL FAIRSTONE CL FAIRLIGHT ROAD MILL LA

CLIFTON GREVILLE ROAD LEEDS CLOSE MANHATTAN GDNS MIDDLE THE BROADWAY BEACON RD FAIRLIGHT ROAD TILEKILN THE HEIGHTS

Brenham Ct AVENUE Surgery NEWMANS RD TESTERS COTTAGES LANE

Ore GRAYSTONE LANE OFFA RD FAIRLIGHT AVENUE LANE

SCHOOL RD ALFRED ROAD CANUTE RD EDITH RD HAMILTON GDNS Bourne / Stream

OLD LONDON ROAD MOSCOW RD BERLIN ROAD SAXON RD ALFRED RD HAROLD RD PINDERS WK 12

BANK CLIVE AV EDMUND RD BARLEY RD HAWTHORN RD 1066 Country Walk Place Farm

SAN JOSE CL BEDFORD RD NEW RD BRACKENDALE VIEW BANK Gate

EDGAR EDWIN ROAD ATHELSTAN RD STAMFORD RD Clive Vale Shear Barn Caravan & Camping Site Wet Wood Long Shaw

Sch GITHA RD LODGE ROAD PINVIEW PINDERS Ecclesbourne Reservoir Covehurst Wood

MUND BOYNE RD BARLEY AV Belmont P Hastings Country Park

GURTH ROAD ROCKLANDS LANE Eastbourne Glen

High Wickham Caravan Site Covehurst Bay

Recreation Ground

Foul Ness

1 2 3 4 5 6

E F G H

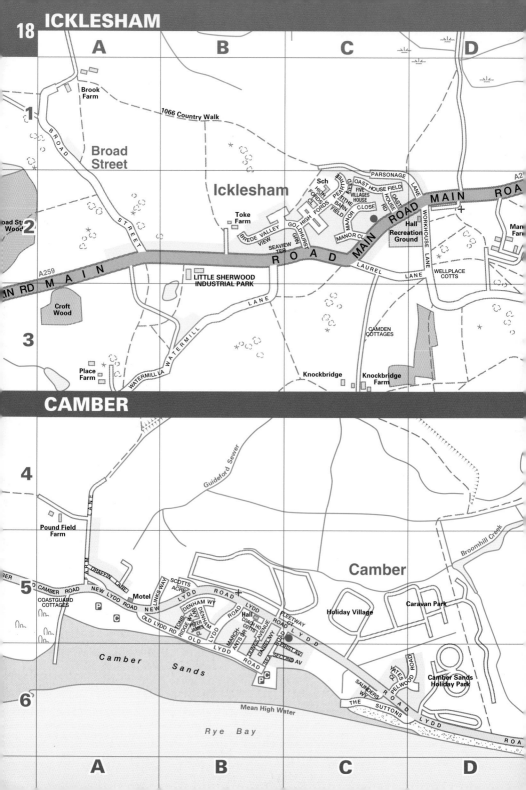

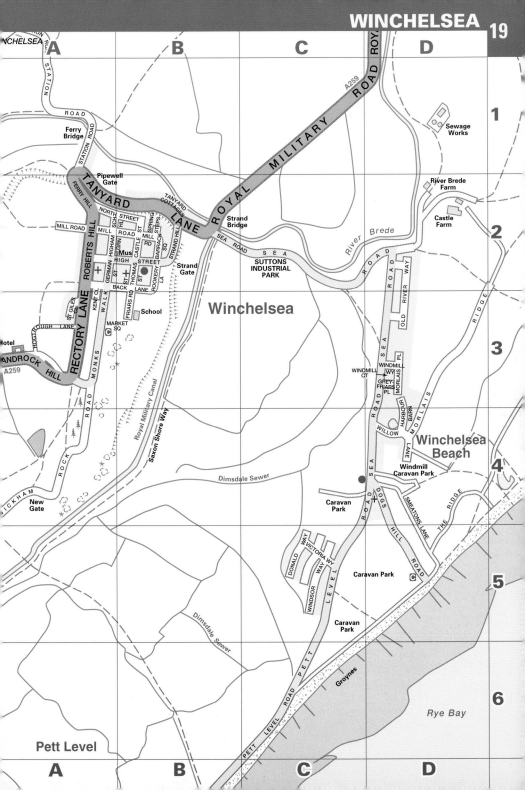

A   B   C   D

1

Sewage
Works

River Brede
Farm

Castle
Farm

2

Ferry
Bridge

Pipewell
Gate

TANYARD LANE

ROYAL MILITARY ROAD

A259

STATION ROAD

FERRY HILL

ROBERTS HILL

RECTORY LANE

TANYARD
COTTAGES

NORTH STREET

MILL ROAD

HIGHAM ST

GERMAN ST

HIGH ST

STRAND HILL

SCH

GRN

CASTLE ST

SPRING ST

MILL RD

BARRACK SQ

STRAND STEPS

ROOKERY LA

THOMAS ST

BACK LANE

FRIARS RD

KENT CL

WALK

MONKS WALK

ST GILES ST

HOGLOUGH LANE

Mus

Strand
Bridge

Strand
Gate

SEA ROAD

SEA ROAD

SUTTONS
INDUSTRIAL
PARK

River Brede

SEA ROAD

OLD RIVER WAY

RIDGE

MORLAIS

Winchelsea

School

MARKET
SQ

Motel

SANDROCK HILL

A259

Royal Military Canal

Saxon Shore Way

ROCK

WICKHAM

New
Gate

Dimsdale Sewer

WINDMILL
CT

WINDMILL
WY

MORLAIS PL

GREY
FRIARS
PL

HARBOUR

BARN

WILLOW

SEA ROAD

DOGS HILL ROAD

SMEATONS LANE

THE RIDGE

PL

LANE

Winchelsea
Beach

Windmill
Caravan Park

3

4

Caravan
Park

Caravan Park

DONALD WAY

VICTORIA WY

WINDSOR WAY

PETT LEVEL ROAD

Caravan Park

Dimsdale Sewer

Groynes

PETT LEVEL ROAD

5

Rye Bay

6

Pett Level

A   B   C   D

The Index includes some names for which there is insufficient space on the maps. These names are indicated by an * and are followed by the nearest adjoining thoroughfare.

Abbey Ct TN33 4 C3
Abbey Dr TN38 14 A6
Abbey Vw TN40 7 E2
Abbey Way TN33 4 E3
Abbots CI TN33 4 E4
Abbotsfield Ct TN34 16 B2
Acorn CI TN37 9 G5
Adams CI TN38 8 D5
Addington CI TN38 14 D4
Adelaide Rd TN38 9 F6
Agincourt CI TN37 9 E2
Albany Rd,
  Bexhill TN40 6 D5
Albany Rd,
  St Leonards TN38 15 F4
Albert Rd, Bexhill TN40 6 D5
Albert Rd,
  Hastings TN34 3 D3
Albourne CI TN38 14 D3
Aldborough Rd TN37 15 G2
Alder CI TN37 9 G4
Alexander Dr TN39 5 B4
Alexandra Rd TN37 15 G3
Alford Way TN40 7 F3
Alfray Rd TN40 7 H3
Alfred Rd TN35 17 E2
Alfred St TN38 15 G4
Alfriston CI TN39 5 B4
All Saints Cres TN35 16 D4
All Saints La TN34 6 C1
All Saints St TN34 3 F3
Allards TN35 12 B1
Allen Way TN40 7 G2
Alma Ter TN37 15 G1
Alma Villas TN37 15 G1
Almonry Flds TN33 4 A3
Alpine Rd TN34 3 E1
Amanda CI TN40 7 G2
Amberstone CI TN34 16 C1
Amherst TN34 15 H2
Amherst Gdns TN34 15 H2
Amherst Rd,
  Bexhill TN40 6 C4
Amherst Rd,
  Hastings TN34 3 A1
Anderida Ct TN39 5 B4
Angela CI TN39 7 G2
Anglesea Ter TN38 15 G3
Ann St TN34 3 D2
Antrona CI TN39 5 B4
Anvil Ct TN37 9 G4
Applewood CI TN37 9 G4
Arbourvale TN38 15 E2
Archery Rd TN38 15 F4
Armstrong CI TN38 8 C5
Arnbury Mews TN38 14 C5
Arnside Rd TN38 14 C5
Arthur Rd TN39 6 B4
Ascot Mews TN38 15 F3
Ashbrook Rd TN37 9 F5
Ashburnham Rd TN35 16 D3
Ashby CI TN39 6 B1
Ashcombe Dr TN39 5 C4
Ashdown CI TN38 14 D1
Ashdown Rd TN40 7 E5
Ashenden Av TN31 20 B3
Ashford Rd TN34 16 A1
Ashford Way TN34 16 A2
Aspen Way TN39 5 B4
Asten CI TN38 14 C4
Asten Flds TN33 4 B3
Athelstan Rd TN35 17 E3
Auckland Rd TN40 7 G4
Augustus Way TN37 9 E3
Austen Way TN35 11 E5
Avondale Rd TN35 15 E2

Back La TN36 19 A2
Badger Gate TN31 20 B3
Badgers Mt TN39 5 D2
Badgers Way TN34 9 H4
Baird Dr TN34 16 A2
Baird Ho TN37 15 G3
Baldslow Down TN37 9 G1
Baldslow Rd TN34 16 B3
Bale CI TN38 5 D3
Bancroft Ho TN39 6 C3
Bancroft Rd TN39 6 C3
Bank Rd TN39 6 D2
Bankside TN31 20 B3
Bargate CI TN39 6 D2
Barham CI TN34 9 H5
Barley Av TN35 17 E4
Barley La TN35 16 D4
Barn Ct TN37 9 G4
Barnfield CI TN34 15 H3
Barnhorn CI TN39 5 B4
Barnhorn Rd TN39 5 A4

Barrack Rd TN40 6 D4
Barrack Sq TN36 19 B2
Barrow Rise TN37 9 G4
Battery Hill TN35 12 B5
Battle Cres TN37 9 F5
Battle Gates TN33 4 A3
Battle Hill TN33 4 E4
Battle Rd TN37 8 D2
Bayencourt North TN40 6 C4
Bayencourt South TN40 6 C4
Beachy Head Vw TN38 8 D2
Beacon Hill TN39 6 A1
Beacon Rd TN35 17 F1
Beaconsfield Rd,
  Bexhill TN40 6 D3
Beaconsfield Rd,
  Hastings TN34 16 B3
Beaneys La TN34 9 H3
Beatrice Walk TN39 6 B3
Beauchamp Rd TN38 9 E5
Beaufort Cres TN37 15 G1
Beaufort Rd TN37 15 G1
Beauharrow Rd TN37 9 E3
Beaulieu Ct TN40 7 G4
Beaulieu Gdns TN37 9 G2
Beaulieu Rd TN38 5 C6
Beauport Gdns TN37 9 E2
Beauport Home Farm
  CI TN37 9 E3
Becket CI TN34 16 B4
Beckley CI TN38 14 B1
Bedford Av TN40 7 E5
Bedford PI TN31 20 C3
Bedford Rd TN35 17 E2
Bedgebury CI TN34 14 C1
Beech CI, Battle TN33 4 B1
Beech CI, Bexhill TN39 5 C1
Beecham PI TN38 8 D4
Beeching CI TN39 6 C2
Beeching Rd TN39 6 C5
Beechwood Gdns TN37 9 H4
Belle Hill TN40 6 D5
Bellingham CI TN37 9 F5
Belmont Rd TN35 16 D4
Belvedere Pk TN35 15 E3
Bembrook Rd TN34 3 F1
Benbow Ho TN39 5 D4
Benenden Rise TN34 16 A1
Berlin Rd TN35 17 E2
Berwick CI TN39 5 B2
Bethune Rd TN39 7 E5
Bethune Way TN34 3 D1
Bevin Ct TN38 9 F6
Bexhill Rd, Bexhill TN38 7 H4
Bexhill Rd,
  St Leonards TN38 14 A6
Bexleigh Av TN39 7 H4
Bicton Gdns TN39 5 D4
Bidwell Av TN39 6 B2
Birch Vw TN39 6 C2
Birch Way TN34 16 A2
Birchington CI TN39 5 C4
Birk Dale TN39 5 C4
Bishops Walk TN40 7 G2
Blackfields Av TN39 6 A3
Blacklands Dr TN34 16 B2
Blackman Av TN38 9 E6
Blackmill CI TN39 6 B1
Blackthorn CI TN37 9 G5
Blackthorn Way TN35 13 E5
Blomfield Rd TN37 15 H3
Bluestone CI TN38 14 D1
Bodiam Av TN40 7 E2
Bodiam Dr TN38 8 B6
Bodle Cres TN39 6 C2
Bohemia Rd TN34 3 A3
Bolebrook Rd TN40 7 E5
Borodales TN39 5 D3
Boscobel Ct TN38 15 E5
Boscobel Rd TN38 15 E4
Boscobel Rd North TN38 15 E4
Bourne Rd*,
  The Bourne TN34 16 C5
Bower TN37 9 F4
Bowmans Dr TN33 4 C2
Bowrey PI TN40 6 C4
Bowsprit Mews TN38 8 D2
Boxgrove CI TN40 7 G4
Boyne Rd TN35 17 E3
Brackendale TN35 17 F2
Brackerne CI TN39 5 B5
Brading CI TN35 16 A3
Bramble Way TN35 13 E6
Brampton CI TN39 6 A5
Brampton CI TN39 6 A5
Branksome Rd TN38 15 E3
Brassey Rd TN39 6 D5
Braybrooke CI TN34 3 B2
Braybrooke Rd TN34 3 B2
Braybrooke Ter TN34 3 B2
Breadsell La TN38 8 A5
Brede CI TN37 8 D2
Brede Valley Vw TN36 18 B2
Brendon Rise TN34 16 D2
Brett Dr TN40 7 G4

Brewery Yd TN33 4 C3
Briar CI TN35 13 F4
Bridge PI TN31 20 C3
Bridge Way TN38 14 B5
Briers Av TN35 9 G6
Briers Gdns TN34 9 G6
Brightling Av TN35 17 F1
Brisco's Walk TN34 3 A2
Bristol Rd TN38 9 E6
Bristol Way TN38 9 E6
Brittany Rd TN38 15 F4
Broad Bucker TN37 9 E3
Broad St TN36 18 A1
Broad Vw TN39 6 A3
Broad Way TN35 13 E5
Broadlands TN35 11 E6
Broadoak La TN39 5 D3
Brockley Rd TN39 6 B5
Brook St TN34 3 D2
Brook Way TN35 10 D6
Brookfield Rd TN40 7 F5
Brookland CI TN34 16 B3
Broomgrove Rd TN34 16 C3
Brunel Rd TN38 8 C6
Buckholt Av TN40 7 G2
Buckholt La TN39 6 C5
Buckhurst PI TN39 6 C5
Buckhurst Rd TN40 6 D5
Buckingham Rd TN38 9 E5
Bulrush PI TN34 14 D2
Bulverhythe Rd TN38 14 B5
Bunting CI TN39 6 E6
Burden PI TN38 9 E6
Burgess Rd TN35 10 D6
Burhill Way TN38 15 E4
Burry Rd TN37 9 G6
Burton Way TN38 15 F5
Burwash CI TN34 10 B6
Bushy Cft TN39 6 A3
Butchers La TN35 11 E1
Buxton Dr TN39 6 C3
Byfields Cft TN39 6 A3
Byways TN37 9 H3
Byworth CI TN35 5 B2

Cadborough Cliff TN31 20 A4
Caldbec Ct TN33 4 C2
Caldbec Hill TN33 4 C2
Calgary Rd TN39 6 C2
Callums Walk TN40 7 F3
Calvert Rd TN34 16 C3
Camber CI TN40 7 F3
Camber Rd,
  Camber TN31 18 A5
Camber Rd, Rye TN31 20 F3
Cambridge Gdns TN34 3 B3
Cambridge Rd,
  Bexhill TN40 6 D3
Cambridge Rd,
  Hastings TN34 3 A3
Camden Cotts TN36 18 C3
Campbell Ct TN38 15 E3
Camperdown St TN39 6 B1
Canada Way TN39 5 D3
Canal Bank TN35 13 G2
Cantelupe Rd TN40 6 D5
Canterbury Rise TN34 16 A1
Canute Rd TN35 17 E2
Caple Ct TN38 9 E5
Caple Gdns TN38 15 F4
Cardiff Rd TN35 15 G4
Cardinals CI TN40 7 G2
Carfax CI TN39 6 C1
Carinus Gdns TN37 9 E4
Carisbrooke Rd TN38 15 F4
Carlisle Par TN34 3 B4
Carmel CI TN39 5 C4
Carnoustie CI TN38 14 D4
Carpenter Dr TN38 8 D5
Carvel Ct TN38 8 D2
Castle Gdns TN34 3 D3
Castle Gdns*,
  Castle Hill Rd TN34 16 B5
Castle Hill Pass TN34 3 D3
Castle Hill Rd TN34 3 D3
Castle St, Hastings TN34 3 D3
Castle St,
  Winchelsea TN36 19 B2
Castle St*,
  Albert Rd TN35 16 B5
Castledown Av TN34 3 E2

Castleham Ind Est
TN38 8 D4
Castleham Rd TN38 8 D4
Catsfield CI TN34 14 C1
Cavendish Av TN38 15 E4
Cavendish PI TN34 3 F2
Caves Rd TN38 15 E5
Cedar CI TN37 9 H4
Celandine Dr TN38 15 E2
Centurion Rise TN34 10 B6
Ceylon Walk TN35 17 E5
Chailey CI TN35 10 A5
Chain La TN33 4 B2
Chalden PI TN39 5 B2

Chalvington Dr TN37 9 G3
Chambers Cres TN38 9 E6
Chambers Rd TN38 9 E6
Chanctonbury Dr TN34 10 A5
Chandler Rd TN39 6 B4
Channel Vw TN40 6 D6
Channel Vw East TN40 6 D6
Channel Vw West TN40 6 D6
Channel Way TN35 12 D6
Chantry Av TN40 6 D3
Chantry CI TN40 6 D3
Chapel Cotts TN33 4 D4
Chapel La,
  Guestling Green TN35 11 H2
Chapel La,
  Westfield TN35 10 C2
Chapel Park Rd TN37 15 G3
Charles Rd TN38 15 F3
Charles Rd West TN38 15 F3
Chartres TN40 7 E3
Chartres CI TN40 7 E3
Chatfield CI TN38 8 D5
Chatham Rd TN37 15 G1
Chelgates TN39 5 B6
Chelsea CI TN40 7 E4
Chelsea Mews*,
  North St TN37 15 G4
Chepbourne Rd TN40 6 C4
Cherry Tree CI TN37 15 G3
Cherry Tree Gdns TN40 7 G2
Chestnut Walk TN39 5 B3
Chichester CI TN39 6 B2
Chichester Ct TN39 5 B3
Chichester Rd TN38 15 F1
Chick Hill TN35 13 G1
Chiltern Dr TN34 16 D2
Chitcombe Walk TN34 10 B6
Chowns Hill TN35 10 B5
Christine CI TN40 7 G2
Church Hill Av TN39 5 C4
Church La,
  Guestling Green TN35 11 H1
Church La,
  Westfield TN35 10 C3
Church Pass TN34 3 F2
Church Pass*,
  Croft Rd TN34 16 C5
Church Rd TN39 6 B2
Church Sq TN31 20 C3
Church St TN40 6 D4
Church Vale Rd TN40 6 D3
Church Wood Dr TN38 14 D1
Church Wood Way TN38 14 D1
Churchfield TN35 10 C3
Churchill Av TN35 11 E6
Churchill Ct TN38 9 F6
Cinque Ports TN38 20 C3
Cinque Ports Way TN38 14 D5
Claremont TN34 3 B3
Claremont Rd TN34 6 C1
Clarence Rd TN37 15 G2
Clarendon CI TN37 9 F5
Claverham CI TN33 4 A3
Claverham Way TN33 4 A3
Clavering Walk TN39 5 A5
Claxton Rd TN40 7 H3
Clement Hill Rd TN34 14 C2
Clevedon Rd TN39 6 B2
Cliff Ct TN38 14 C5
Cliff End La TN35 13 C2
Cliff Way TN35 13 E5
Clifford Rd TN40 6 D5
Clifton CI TN34 3 A3
Clifton PI TN31 20 C3
Clifton Rd TN35 17 E1
Clifton Rise TN40 7 H3
Cliftonville Rd TN38 14 B5
Cliftonville Rd TN38 14 C5
Clinch Green Av TN39 6 A1
Clinton Cres TN38 15 F3
Clinton Way TN35 13 E5
Clive Av TN35 9 F4
Cloudesley Rd TN37 15 G3
Clover Lea TN34 10 A5
Clyde Rd TN38 15 G4
Coach House Cotts TN31 18 B5
Coastguard Cotts TN31 18 A5
Coastguard La TN35 12 B5
Cobourg PI TN34 3 F2
Cockcrow Wood TN37 9 H4
Coghurst Rd TN35 17 E1
Colebrook Rd TN39 6 B5
College Rd TN40 7 F4
Collett CI TN38 9 E4
Collier Rd TN34 3 F1
Collington Av TN39 6 A5
Collington Grove TN39 5 D4
Collington La East TN39 5 D4
Collington La West TN39 5 D4
Collington Park Cres TN39 6 A4
Collington Rise TN39 5 D3
Collinstone Rd TN38 15 E4
Collinswood Dr TN38 15 E4
Combermere Rd TN38 15 F3
Commanders Walk TN35 12 D6

Compton CI TN40 7 F4
Conduit Hill TN31 20 C3
Coneyburrow Gdns TN38 8 C5
Coneyburrow La TN39 5 A2
Conifer CI TN34 16 B1
Conqueror Rd TN38 14 C4
Constable Way TN40 7 E3
Cooden CI TN39 5 B6
Cooden Dr TN39 5 B6
Cooden Ledge TN38 8 D2
Cooden Sea Rd TN39 5 B6
Cookham Dene TN40 6 D5
Cookson Gdns TN35 16 D1
Cooper Dr TN39 6 B1
Cooper Rd TN31 20 A3
Cooper Rise TN37 9 E4
Copper Beeches TN37 9 G5
Copse CI TN38 8 C6
Copse Rd TN39 5 D4
Cornfield Ter TN37 15 G2
Cornwall Rd TN39 6 C5
Cornwallis Gdns TN34 3 B3
Cornwallis St TN34 3 B3
Cornwallis Ter TN34 3 B3
Coronation Gdns TN33 4 E3
Cotswold CI TN34 16 D1
Cottage La TN35 10 C1
Courthope Dr TN39 5 D3
Courthouse St TN34 3 F2
Coventry Rd TN39 9 F6
Coverdale Av TN39 5 B5
Cowden Walk TN38 15 E1
Cowdray CI TN39 5 C2
Cowdray Park Rd TN39 5 B2
Cranbrook Rd TN37 15 G2
Cranfield Rd TN40 6 D5
Cranleigh CI TN39 6 B5
Cranston Av TN39 6 A5
Cranston CI TN39 6 A4
Cranston Rise TN39 6 A5
Crecy CI TN37 9 E2
Croft Rd TN34 3 F1
Crofton Park Av TN39 5 D4
Cromer Walk TN34 16 B3
Cross St TN37 15 G4
Crowborough Rd TN39 11 F6
Crowhurst La TN39 6 D1
Crowhurst Rd,
  Battle TN33 8 A6
Crowhurst Rd,
  St Leonards TN38 14 B1
Crowmere Av TN40 6 D3
Crowmere Ter TN40 6 D3
Crown La TN34 16 C5
Cubitt Way TN38 8 C5
Cuckfield CI TN37 9 G3
Cumberland Gdns TN38 15 F3
Cumberland Rd TN39 6 C1
Curlew Ct TN38 8 C6
Cuthbert CI TN39 6 B1
Cypress CI TN38 15 E4
Cyprus PI TN31 20 B3

Dalehurst Rd TN39 6 B2
Dallington CI TN40 7 H3
Dalmeny Rd TN40 6 A4
Dane Court CI TN39 6 C3
Dane Rd TN38 15 F3
Daniel Way TN31 18 B6
Daresbury CI TN39 6 B3
Darwell CI TN39 14 C2
Davis CI TN39 6 B1
De Cham Av TN37 15 H3
De Cham Rd TN37 15 G3
De Chardin Dr TN34 10 B5
De La Warr Mews TN40 6 D5
De La Warr Par TN40 6 D6
De La Warr Rd TN40 7 E4
De Moleyns CI TN40 7 E4
Deadmans La TN31 20 C2
Deans CI TN39 6 B2
Deans Dr TN39 6 B2
Deepdene Gdns TN35 16 D2
Deerswood La TN39 5 D3
Delaware Dr TN38 8 D3
Dell CI TN38 15 E1
Denbigh CI TN39 5 D3
Denbigh Rd TN39 5 D3
Denehurst Gdns TN35 10 C5
Denham TN38 8 D5
Denham Way TN31 18 B5
Denmark PI TN34 3 C3
Denton CI TN31 20 B2
Devonshire Rd,
  Bexhill TN40 6 D5
Devonshire Rd,
  Hastings TN34 3 C3
Devonshire Sq TN40 6 D5
Diana CI TN39 7 G2
Ditchling Dr TN35 11 F6
Dittons Mews TN38 14 C1
Dogs Hill Rd TN36 19 D4
Donald Way TN36 19 C5
Donric PI TN38 9 E5
Dordrecht Way TN34 16 A3

Dorset Pl TN34 3 B3
Dorset Rd TN40 7 E6
Dorset Rd South TN40 7 E5
Douce Gro TN38 15 E2
Douchs Pass*,
  The Bourne TN34 16 C5
Down Rd TN39 6 B3
Downey Cl TN37 9 F3
Downlands Av TN39 6 B5
Downlands Cl TN39 6 B4
Downs Rd TN34 16 A2
Draffin La TN31 18 A5
Drapers Way TN38 15 F1
Drayton Rise TN39 5 C4
Drury La TN38 15 E1
Dudley Rd TN35 16 D3
Duke Mews*,
Duke St TN37 15 F1
Duke Rd TN37 15 F1
Duke St, Bexhill TN38 6 A4
Duke St,
  St Leonards TN37 15 F1
Duke Ter TN37 15 G1
Dukes Hill TN33 4 C2
Dunclutha Rd TN34 16 B1
Dunes Av TN31 18 B6
Dymond Rd TN38 9 E6

Eagle Rd TN31 20 C3
Earl St TN34 3 C2
East Ascent TN38 15 F5
East Beach St TN33 3 F3
East Bourne St*,
  The Bourne TN34 16 C5
East Hill Pass TN34 16 D5
East Par TN34 3 E3
East St, Hastings TN34 3 F3
East St, Rye TN31 20 C3
East St,
  St Leonards TN37 15 G4
Eastgate St TN39 5 C2
Eastway TN39 5 C4
Eastwood Rd TN39 6 B4
Ebden's Hill TN37 9 F2
Ebenezer Rd TN34 16 D5
Eden Dr TN39 5 D3
Edgar Rd TN35 17 E3
Edinburgh Rd,
  Bexhill TN40 6 C4
Edinburgh Rd,
  St Leonards TN38 14 C4
Edith Rd TN35 17 F2
Edmonton Rd TN39 6 C2
Edmund Rd TN35 17 E3
Edward Rd TN37 15 H4
Edward Ter TN38 9 E5
Edwin Rd TN35 17 E3
Effingham Dr TN39 5 C4
Egerton Rd TN39 6 B6
Egremont Pl TN34 16 D5
Eight Acre La TN35 11 F1
Eisenhower Dr TN38 8 D3
Elderwood Cl TN39 6 D1
Eldridge Way TN37 9 G3
Eleanor Ter TN35 17 F1
Elizabeth Rd TN38 15 E1
Ellenslea Rd TN37 15 G4
Ellerslie La TN39 6 A2
Ellis Cl TN34 3 A3
Elms La TN35 13 E1
Elmstead Rd TN40 7 E3
Elphinstone Av TN34 16 B2
Elphinstone Gdns TN34 16 B2
Elphinstone Rd TN34 10 C6
Elsted Rd TN39 5 D4
Emmanuel Rd TN34 3 E1
Endwell Rd TN40 6 D5
Epsom Cl TN38 15 F3
Eridge Cl TN39 6 A5
Essenden Rd TN38 15 E5
Essex Rd TN35 9 E5
Eversfield Pl TN37 3 A4
Eversley Cl TN37 15 G1
Eversley Cres TN37 15 G1
Eversley Ct TN37 15 G1
Eversley Rd, Bexhill TN40 6 D6
Eversley Rd,
  St Leonards TN37 15 G1
Ewhurst Cl TN34 16 A1
Exmouth Pl TN34 3 F3

Fair Mdw TN31 20 C2
Fairfax Av TN38 8 D2
Fairfield Chase TN39 6 A4
Fairfield Rd TN37 9 G3
Fairlight Av TN35 17 F1
Fairlight Cl TN40 7 H3
Fairlight Gdns TN35 13 E5
Fairlight Rd,
  Hastings TN35 12 A5
Fairlight Rd,
  Hastings TN35 17 F1
Fairmount Rd TN40 7 E4
Fairstone Cl TN35 17 F1
Falaise Rd, Hastings TN34 3 A3
Falaise Rd,
  Hastings TN34 15 H4
Falconbury Dr TN39 5 C5
Falconers Dr TN33 4 E3
Farley Bank TN35 16 D3
Farley Way TN35 12 D5
Farm La TN31 18 A5

Farmlands Cl TN37 9 G3
Faygate Cl TN39 6 C1
Fearon Rd TN34 16 A3
Fellows Rd TN34 16 C2
Fen Ct TN38 14 D2
Fern Rd TN38 15 E2
Fernlea Cl TN35 10 C1
Fernside Av TN38 14 D3
Ferring Cl TN31 20 B3
Ferry Hill TN36 19 A2
Ferry Rd TN31 20 B3
Festival Gdns TN38 6 D1
Field Way TN38 14 C3
Filsham Dr TN40 7 H2
Filsham Rd TN38 14 D5
Filsham Valley TN38 15 E4
Findon Cl TN39 5 D5
Finley Cl TN38 14 D5
Firehills Cotts TN35 12 B6
Firle Cl TN35 17 F1
Firle Rd TN39 5 C4
First Av, Bexhill TN40 7 G3
First Av, Rye TN31 18 B6
Firtree Cl TN38 5 B5
Firtree Rd TN34 16 C2
Fishmarket Rd TN31 20 C3
Fishponds La TN31 10 D3
Five Villages Ho TN35 18 C2
Fleetway Ct TN31 18 B5
Fletcher Av TN37 9 E2
Flimwell Cl TN38 8 C6
Florida Cl TN38 14 D5
Folkington Gdns TN37 9 G3
Fontwell Av TN39 5 B2
Ford Rd TN38 15 E1
Forest Way TN34 3 B1
Forge Way TN37 9 G4
Fowlers Cl TN35 5 D3
Foxcote TN37 9 H4
Foxhill TN38 5 D2
Francis Bird Pl TN38 9 G3
Frant Av TN39 5 B3
Frant Cl TN39 5 B2
Frederick Rd TN35 16 D1
Freshfields TN38 14 A5
Freshwater Av TN34 16 A2
Frewyn Cl TN38 5 B5
Friars Hill TN35 11 H4
Friars Rd TN36 19 B3
Friars Way TN34 16 B1
Fryatts Way TN39 6 A3
Fulford Cl TN39 15 E3
Fyning Pl TN39 5 B3
Fyrsway TN35 12 D6

Gainsborough Rd TN40 7 F3
Galley Hill Vw TN40 7 F5
Ganton Cl TN38 14 D3
Garden Cl TN40 6 D5
Gardner Way TN38 15 F5
Garth Cl TN39 5 B6
Gatehouse Cl TN39 5 B6
Gatelands Dr TN39 6 B3
Gavin Astor Cl TN40 7 G3
Geary Pl TN31 10 C2
Gensing Rd TN38 15 G4
George Mews TN33 4 C3
George St TN34 3 E3
Georgian Cl TN37 7 E3
Georgian Walk TN38 14 D3
German St TN36 19 A2
Ghyllside Av TN34 9 G5
Ghyllside Dr TN34 9 G5
Ghyllside Way TN34 9 H5
Gibb Cl TN40 7 F2
Gilbert Rd TN38 15 F3
Gillham Wood Rd TN39 5 C5
Gillsmans Dr TN38 15 E2
Gillsmans Hill TN38 14 D2
Gillsmans Pk TN38 14 D3
Githa Rd TN35 17 E3
Gladstone Ter TN34 3 E1
Glassenbury Dr TN40 7 G4
Glebe Cl TN39 5 C4
Glenburn TN39 6 D1
Gleneagles Cl TN40 7 F4
Gleneagles Dr TN38 14 D4
Glengorse TN33 4 E4
Glengorse Ct TN33 4 E4
Glenleigh Av TN39 6 A2
Glenleigh Park Rd TN39 6 A2
Glenthorn Rd TN39 6 B4
Glenview Cl TN35 17 E3
Gloucester Av TN40 7 H4
Glovers La TN39 6 D2
Glynde Ct TN39 5 B4
Glyndebourne Gdns
  TN37 9 G3
Glyne Ascent TN40 7 F4
Glyne Barn Cl TN40 7 H3
Glyne Dr TN40 7 G3
Godwin Rd TN35 16 D3
Goldhurst Grn TN36 18 C2
Goodwood Cl TN40 6 D2
Gordon Pl TN39 3 E1
Gordon Rd TN35 16 D3
Gorsethorn Way TN35 12 D6
Grand Av TN40 7 G3
Grand Par TN37,38 15 G5
Grange Court Dr TN39 6 C3
Grange Rd TN34 10 A6

Graystone La TN35 17 E2
Grazebrook Cl TN39 5 B4
Green La TN39 5 C3
Greenacres TN35 10 C3
Greenfields Cl TN37 9 F3
Greenways TN39 6 A1
Grenada Cl TN39 5 C4
Grenham Ct TN35 9 F2
Gresham Way TN38 15 E3
Gresley Rd TN38 8 D4
Greville Rd TN35 17 E1
Greyfriars Pl TN36 19 D3
Greyhorses TN39 5 A4
Grosvenor Cres TN38 14 D5
Grosvenor Rd TN38 14 D5
Grove Rd TN35 17 E1
Guldeford Rd TN31 20 E2
Gunters La TN39 6 B2
Gurth Rd TN35 17 E3
Gwyneth Gro TN40 7 G2

Hadrian Gdns TN37 9 E3
Halton Cres TN34 16 D3
Halton Pl TN34 16 D3
Halton Ter TN34 16 D3
Hamilton Gdns TN35 17 F2
Hamilton Ter TN39 5 D4
Hampden Cl TN33 4 A3
Hanover Cl TN40 6 D4
Harbour Barn TN36 19 D4
Harbour Rd TN31 20 C4
Harbour Way TN38 8 C2
Hardrada Rise TN34 9 H6
Hardwicke Rd TN34 16 D3
Hare Way TN37 9 G4
Harewood Cl TN39 6 A5
Harkness Dr TN34 10 D6
Harlequin Gdns TN37 9 E3
Harley Shute Rd TN38 14 C5
Harley Way TN38 14 C5
Harmony Wood TN35 10 A4
Harold Mews TN38 15 G5
Harold Pl TN34 3 C3
Harold Rd TN35 16 D3
Harold Ter TN33 4 E4
Harrier La TN33 4 F3
Harriet La TN37 9 F3
Hartfield Mdw TN38 8 C6
Hartfield Rd TN39 5 C6
Harting Combe TN38 15 F3
Hartwood Lodge TN40 6 D5
Harvest Way TN37 9 G4
Harvey Cl TN38 8 D5
Haslam Cres TN40 7 G3
Hassell Rd, Battle TN33 4 F4
Hastings Rd,
  Bexhill TN40 7 E4
Hatherley Rd TN37 15 G4
Havelock Rd,
  Bexhill TN40 6 D3
Havelock Rd,
  Hastings TN34 3 C3
Haven Rd TN38 14 B5
Hawkhurst Way TN39 5 C5
Hawthorn Av TN39 5 C4
Hawthorn Rd TN37 17 F2
Haywood Way TN38 10 D6
Hazelwood Cl TN39 5 B4
Hazelwood Gdns TN37 9 H4
Heather Way TN35 13 E6
Heatherdune Rd TN39 6 B3
Heathfield Cl TN34 10 C3
Heathlands TN35 10 C3
Heighton Cl TN39 5 D4
Helensdene Walk TN37 15 G3
Henderson Cl TN34 16 A2
Henley Cl TN31 20 A3
Henry Ter*,
  All Saints St TN34 16 D5
Herbrand Walk TN39 5 A6
Heron Cl TN38 14 C3
Hertford Cl TN38 9 E5
Hever Cres TN39 6 A3
Hickman Way TN34 9 H5
High Bank TN35 17 E2
High Bank Cl TN35 16 D2
High Beech Cl TN38 8 D3
High Branches TN39 5 D3
High Fords TN36 18 C2
High Fords Cl TN36 18 C2
High St, Battle TN33 4 C3
High St, Bexhill TN40 6 D4
High St, Hastings TN34 3 D3
High St, Rye TN31 20 C3
High St,
  Winchelsea TN36 19 A2
High Wickham TN35 16 D4
Higham Gdns TN35 11 H2
Higham Grn TN36 19 A2
Highfield Dr TN38 8 C6
Highfield Gdns TN38 6 D2
Highgrove TN33 4 A3
Highlands Dr TN34 16 B1
Highlands Cl TN38 15 F4
Highlands Gdns TN38 15 F4
Highview Cl TN37 9 H4
Highwater Vw TN38 8 D2
Highwood Av TN39 5 B1
Highwoods Ct TN39 5 D3
Hilders Cliff TN31 20 C3
Hill TN35 12 B5

Hill St TN34 3 F3
Hillborough Cl TN39 5 C3
Hillcrest TN31 20 C1
Hillcrest Av TN39 6 B2
Hillside Rd, Bexhill TN40 6 D4
Hillside Rd,
  Hastings TN34 9 H3
Hilltop Dr TN31 20 C1
Hillyfield TN31 20 C2
Hillyglen Cl TN34 3 A2
Hoads Wood Rd TN34 16 B1
Hogtrough La TN36 19 A3
Hole Farm Cl TN34 16 A2
Holland Av TN39 5 B4
Holliers Hill TN40 6 D2
Hollingburst Cl TN37 9 F4
Hollingburst Rd TN37 9 F5
Hollington Ct TN38 15 E3
Hollington Old La TN38 14 B5
Hollington Park Rd TN38 15 E2
Hollington Park Rd TN38 15 E2
Holly Cl TN35 5 B1
Hollybank Gdns TN35 15 F2
Holm Oak TN35 5 D5
Holmesdale Gdns TN34 3 A3
Holmesdale Rd TN40 6 B5
Holmhurst La TN37 9 F3
Homelands Cl TN39 6 B2
Honeysuckle Cl TN37 9 H4
Honies Cl TN39 6 C3
Hoover Cl TN38 8 D2
Hop Garden Cl TN34 3 A2
Hopgarden Cl TN34 9 H6
Hornrye Pk TN37 15 H3
Hornrye Rd TN37 15 H3
Hornrye Rd TN37 15 G2
Horseshoe Cl TN38 15 F1
Howard Ho TN39 5 B3
Howards Cres TN39 5 B3
Howlett Cl TN38 8 D5
Hughenden Pl TN34 16 B3
Hughenden Rd TN34 16 B3
Hunting Cl TN40 6 D4
Hurrell Rd TN34 16 D2
Hurst Way TN35 10 B5
Hurstwood Cl TN40 7 H3
Hylands Yd*,
  The Mint TN31 20 C3
Hythe Av TN38 14 A6

Ian Cl TN40 7 G2
Icklesham Dr TN38 8 B6
Iden Ct TN34 9 H6
Ingleside TN38 8 C5
Inglewood Gdns TN38 8 C5
Ingrams Av TN39 6 D1
Ironlatch Av TN38 14 D2
Ironlatch Cl TN38 14 D1
Isherwood TN33 4 B2
Ivyhouse La TN35 10 D6

Jacobs Acre TN40 6 D3
Jameson Cres TN38 9 E6
Jameson Rd TN40 6 D5
Jarretts Cl TN31 20 C3
Jarvis Brook Cl TN38 5 C5
Jasmine Way TN39 6 B5
Jefferson Way TN38 8 D3
Jenners La TN35 11 F4
Jevington Cl TN35 5 C6
John MaCadam Way
  TN37 9 E3
Johnson Cl TN38 8 D3
Jubilee Rd TN38 6 A1
Junction Rd TN31 9 F2
Juniper Cl TN38 8 C5

Katkins Path TN34 3 D2
Keats Cl TN38 14 D5
Kenilworth Rd TN38 15 F4
Kennedy Cl TN38 9 F6
Kennedy Rd TN38 7 F4
Kennel La TN39 5 B4
Kensington Cl TN38 8 C6
Kent Cl, Bexhill TN40 7 H4
Kent Cl,
  Winchelsea TN36 19 A3
Kent Rd TN38 8 D5
Kenton Cl TN39 6 B3
Kenwood Cl TN34 16 C1
Keppel Rd TN34 16 A2
Kestrel Cl TN40 7 E4
Keymer Cl TN34 14 D6
Kildare Cl TN34 10 C6
Kiln Dr TN31 20 C1
King Edward Av TN34 9 G5
King Edward Cl TN34 9 G6
King Offa Way TN34 6 C4
Kings Av TN34 20 D2
Kings Cl TN40 6 A1
Kings Rd TN37 15 G4
Kings Walk TN34 3 C3
Kingscott Cl TN39 6 B1
Kingsdale Cl, Battle TN34 4 E4
Kingsdale Cl,
  St Leonards TN37 9 E4
Kingsley Cl TN34 9 E4
Kingswood Av TN39 6 A2
Kinver La TN37 7 H3
Kite Cl TN38 14 D3
Kites Nest Walk TN39 5 B3
Knebworth Rd TN39 6 A4

Knights Mdw TN33 4 E3
Knole Rd TN40 7 E6
Knoll Rise TN38 15 E4
Knowle Av TN35 12 D5
Knowle Cl TN38 15 F2
Knowle Ct TN38 12 D5

Laburnum Gdns TN40 7 F3
Lake House Cl TN39 5 C4
Laleham Cl TN37 9 G4
Lancaster Rd TN39 9 E4
Lancing Cl TN34 9 H6
Landgate TN31 20 C3
Landgate Sq TN31 20 C3
Langham Cl TN34 16 B1
Langham Rd TN34 16 B1
Langley Cl TN39 6 C1
Langton Cl TN33 4 E3
Lansdowne Way TN40 7 E3
Larkhill TN40 6 D4
Laton Rd TN34 16 A3
Laurel La TN34 18 C2
Laurel Walk TN38 8 C6
Lavant Cl TN39 5 B2
Lavender Walk TN31 20 C2
Lea Av TN31 20 A3
Leasam La TN31 20 B1
Leasingham Gdns TN39 6 B3
Ledsham Av TN37 9 F4
Ledsham Cl TN37 9 F4
Ledsham Pk TN37 9 F4
Ledsham Way TN37 9 F4
Leedes Cl TN35 17 F1
Leopold Rd TN39 6 C4
Lesley Cl TN40 7 G2
Lewes Cl TN39 6 A5
Lewins Ct TN33 4 C2
Lewis Av TN40 7 H4
Lewis Cl TN39 9 E6
Leybourne Gdns TN37 9 G3
Lime Cl TN38 15 F2
Lincoln Cl TN38 9 E5
Linden Rd TN40 6 C5
Links Dr TN40 7 E4
Links Way TN31 18 A5
Linley Cl, Bexhill TN40 7 F6
Linley Cl, Hastings TN34 16 C2
Linley Dr TN34 16 B2
Linton Cres TN34 3 A2
Linton Rd TN34 3 A2
Lion St TN31 20 C3
Lionel Rd TN37 7 E5
Little Common Rd TN39 5 C3
Little Ridge Av TN37 9 F3
Little Sherwood Ind Pk
  TN36 18 B2
Little Twitten TN39 5 B5
Lodge Rd TN35 17 E3
London Rd, Battle TN34 4 C1
London Rd, Bexhill TN39 6 C4
London Rd,
  St Leonards TN37 15 F1
Long Av TN40 7 G3
Longacre Cl TN37 9 G3
Lords La TN35 17 F1
Lovat Mead TN38 14 C5
Love La TN31 20 B2
Lower Glen Rd TN37 9 F5
Lower Lake TN33 4 D3
Lower Park Rd TN34 16 B1
Lower South Rd TN37 15 G2
Lower Waites La TN35 13 E5
Loxwood Cl TN39 5 C2
Lucy Way TN39 6 B3
Lullington Cl TN40 7 G3
Lullington Gdns TN37 9 G3
Lychgates Cl TN40 7 E3
Lydd Rd TN31 18 B6
Lyndhurst Av TN34 16 C1
Lynwood Cl TN37 9 H4
Lytham Cl TN38 15 E3

Maberley Rd TN40 6 D2
Madeira Dr TN34 9 G6
Magdalen Rd,
  Bexhill TN40 6 D5
Magdalen Rd,
  St Leonards TN37 15 H3
Magpie Cl, Bexhill TN39 5 B2
Magpie Cl,
  St Leonards TN38 14 C3
Main Rd, Hastings TN35 10 C2
Main Rd,
  Icklesham TN35,TN36 18 A3
Maitland Cl TN34 10 A5
Malvern Way TN34 16 D1
Manhattan Gdns TN37 17 F1
Mann St TN34 3 C2
Manor Cl TN36 18 C2
Manor Rd, Bexhill TN40 7 E4
Manor Rd,
  Hastings TN34 5 B4
Mansell Cl TN38 5 B4
Manston Way TN34 16 A3
Maple Av TN39 5 B5
Maple Cl TN38 5 B5
Maple Walk TN38 5 B5
Mapleheights TN37 9 F2
Maplehurst Cl TN37 9 F2
Maplehurst Rd TN37 9 F2

Marchants Dr TN31 18 B6
Marcus Gdns TN37 9 E4
Mare Bay Cl TN38 8 C2
Marianne Pk TN35 16 D3
Marina, Bexhill TN40 6 D6
Marina,
St Leonards TN38 15 E5
Marina Court Av TN40 6 D6
Marine Ct TN38 15 G5
Marine Par TN34 3 E3
Market Rd, Battle TN33 4 C3
Market Rd, Rye TN31 20 C3
Market Sq, Battle TN33 4 C3
Market Sq,
Winchelsea TN36 19 A3
Market St, Rye TN31 20 C3
Market St,
St Leonards TN38 15 G5
Markwick Ct TN38 15 F3
Markwick Ter TN38 15 F3
Marlborough Cl TN38 15 E2
Marley Cl TN38 4 F3
Marley Gdns TN33 4 F3
Marley La TN33 4 F3
Marley Rd TN31 20 B3
Marley Rise TN33 4 E3
Marline Av TN38 9 E5
Marline Rd TN38 9 E5
Marlow Dr TN37 9 G4
Martello Cl TN31 20 B4
Martineau La TN35 11 G5
Martingale Ct TN37 9 G4
Martletts TN40 7 F4
Martyns Way TN40 7 G3
Mason Rd TN31 20 B3
Maudlin Ct TN37 15 G3
Maunsell Rd TN38 8 D4
Mayfair Mews,
Bexhill TN40 6 D3
Mayfair Mews,
St Leonards TN38 15 E1
Mayfield La TN38 14 B1
Mayfield Way TN40 7 E3
Mayne Way TN34 10 C6
Mayo La TN39 6 B1
Maytree Gdns TN40 7 F3
Maze Hill TN38 15 F4
Maze Hill Ter TN38 15 F4
Meadow Bank TN33 4 E3
Meadow Cl TN38 9 D1
Meadow Cres TN39 6 D1
Meadow Vw TN35 10 C2
Meadow Way TN35 12 D5
Meadowsweet Cl TN38 14 C2
Meads Av TN39 5 B4
Meads Rd TN39 5 B4
Medina Ter TN38 15 G5
Mendip Gdns TN34 16 D1
Menzies Rd TN38 15 E1
Mercatoria TN38 15 G5
Mermaid Pass TN31 20 C3
Mermaid St TN31 20 C3
Merrimede Cl TN38 15 E4
Meryon Ct TN31 20 C3
Mews Rd TN38 15 G5
Michele Cl TN38 15 F2
Michelson Cl TN38 8 D5
Middle Rd TN35 17 F1
Middle St TN34 3 C3
Middlesex Rd TN40 7 E5
Mildenhall Dr TN37 9 F6
Military Rd TN31 20 C2
Mill Cl, Hastings TN35 17 G1
Mill Cl, Westfield TN35 10 C1
Mill La,
Bachelors Bump TN35 11 F5
Mill La, Westfield TN35 10 C1
Mill Rd, Rye TN31 20 C1
Mill Rd,
Winchelsea TN36 19 A2
Mill View Rd TN39 6 C1
Milland Cl TN40 7 F3
Millfield Rise TN40 6 A3
Millham Cl TN39 6 A3
Milward Cres TN34 3 E2
Milward Rd TN34 3 D2
Minsted Sq TN39 5 B6
Mistley Cl TN40 7 H2
Mitre Way TN33 4 E3
Mitten Rd TN40 6 D4
Moat La TN33 10 A3
Monarch Gdns TN37 9 E4
Monks Walk TN36 19 A3
Montana Ct TN37 8 D3
Monterey Cl TN39 5 D5
Monterey Gdns TN39 5 D5
Montgomery Rd TN35 11 F6
Moor La TN35 10 C2
Moorhurst Cl TN38 8 D4
Morgan Cl TN39 6 C1
Morlais Pl TN36 19 D3
Morlais Ridge TN36 19 D3
Moscow Rd TN35 17 E2
Mount Idol Vw TN39 6 A1
Mount Joy TN33 4 D3
Mount Pleasant Cres
TN34 16 B3
Mount Pleasant Ct TN34 16 C3
Mount Pleasant Rd TN34 16 C3
Mount Rd TN38 17 E2
Mount St TN33 4 C3

Mountbatten Cl TN35 11 F6
Muirfield Rise TN38 14 D4
Mulberry Cl TN39 5 B4
Mulberry Walk TN37 9 H4

Napier Rd TN38 8 C4
Nelson Ho TN39 5 D4
Nelson Rd TN34 3 D1
Netherfield Rd TN33 4 B1
Netherwood Cl TN34 10 A5
New Cut TN35 10 C2
New England La TN31 20 C1
New Lydd Rd TN31 18 A5
New Moorsite TN35 10 D3
New Park Av TN40 6 D4
New Rd, Fairlight TN35 12 C5
New Rd, Hastings TN35 17 F2
New Rd, Rye TN31 20 D3
New Winchelsea Rd
TN31 20 C4
Newgate Rd TN37 15 G2
Newhaven Walk TN38 9 E6
Newlands Av TN39 6 B3
Newlands Cl TN34 10 A5
Newmans Way TN35 17 F1
Newts Way TN36 14 C2
Ninfield Rd TN39 6 B1
Nook Cl TN35 17 F1
Norfolk Cl TN39 6 C1
Norfolk Dr TN39 9 E4
Norman Cl TN33 4 E3
Norman Rd TN37 15 G5
Normandale TN39 6 A5
Normandy Rd TN34 9 G6
North Rd, Bexhill TN39 6 C1
North Rd,
St Leonards TN37 15 G2
North Salts TN31 20 D2
North St,
St Leonards TN38 15 G5
North St,
Winchelsea TN36 19 A2
North Ter TN34 16 D3
North Trade Rd TN33 4 A3
Northampton Way TN38 9 E5
Northiam Rise TN38 14 C1
Northolt Pl TN34 3 B3
Nutley Cl TN31 20 B3

Oak Rd TN40 6 C4
Oakfield Rd TN35 16 D2
Oakfield Way TN39 5 B2
Oakhurst Cl TN34 10 A5
Oakhurst Rd TN34 4 D1
Oaklea Cl TN37 9 G5
Oakleigh Rd TN38 9 G4
Oakwood Av TN39 6 C2
Oakwood Cl TN34 16 B1
Oast House Cl TN34 9 H4
Oast House Dr TN31 20 A4
Oast House Fld TN36 18 C2
Oast House Rd TN36 18 C2
Oban Rd TN37 9 G6
Ochiltree Cl TN34 10 C6
Ochiltree Rd TN34 10 C6
Ocklynge TN39 5 C3
Ockman La TN31 20 C3
Offa Rd TN35 17 E1
Old Brickyard TN31 20 A3
Old Church Rd TN34 9 E4
Old Farm Rd TN39 6 A4
Old Harrow Rd TN37 9 F6
Old House Gdns TN34 16 B1
Old Humphrey Av*,
All Saints St TN34 16 D4
Old Ladies Ct TN33 4 C3
Old London Rd TN35 16 D4
Old Lydd Rd TN31 18 A5
Old Manor Cl TN40 7 E4
Old Mill Pk TN39 6 B3
Old Mill Walk TN33 4 C3
Old River Way TN36 19 D3
Old Roar Rd TN37 9 F5
Old Top Rd TN35 17 F1
Oliver Cl TN34 3 A3
Olivers Mews TN33 4 D4
Orchard Cl TN40 6 D4
Orchard Rd TN40 6 D2
Ore TN34 10 B6
Ormerod Av TN38 9 E5
Osbern Cl TN39 5 C5
Osborne Ct TN34 16 A2
Oxford Rd TN38 9 E6
Oxford Ter*,
Tackleway TN34 16 D5

Paddock Cl TN40 6 D3
Paddock Rd TN37 9 G4
Pages Av TN39 6 A6
Pages La TN39 5 D5
Pankhurst Cl TN39 6 B1
Pankhurst Rise TN39 6 B1
Pannel La TN35 12 D1
Park Av, Bexhill TN39 6 C6
Park Av, Hastings TN34 9 H6
Park Cl TN34 9 H6
Park Cres TN34 9 H6
Park La, Battle TN33 4 C3
Park La, Bexhill TN39 6 B3
Park Rd TN34 6 C5
Park View Rd TN35 10 C1
Park View Ter*,
Cottage La TN35 10 C1
Park Vw TN34 9 H6
Park Way TN34 9 H6
Park Wood Rd TN34 10 A5
Parker Rd TN34 16 C2
Parkhurst Rd TN34 6 C5
Parks Yd TN33 4 C3
Parkstone Rd TN34 9 H6
Parkstone Ter TN34 9 H5
Parsonage La,
Hastings TN35 10 A2
Parsonage La,
Winchelsea TN36 18 C2
Parsons Cl TN38 8 D5
Paton Rd TN39 6 A1
Paxhill Cl TN38 8 D5
Paynton Rd TN37 9 F6
Peartree Fld TN36 18 C2
Peartree La TN39 5 C3
Pebsham Dr TN40 7 G2
Pebsham La TN40 7 F3
Pegwell Cl TN34 16 A3
Pelham Dr TN33 4 D3
Pelham Pl TN34 3 D3
Pelham St TN34 3 C3
Pelwood Rd TN31 18 C6
Pembury Gro TN39 6 B2
Penhurst Cl TN37 9 G2
Penhurst Dr TN40 7 G2
Penland Rd TN40 7 F3
Pennine Rise TN34 16 D1
Penny La TN40 7 G3
Pentland Cl TN39 9 G4
Percy Rd TN35 17 E1
Perth Rd TN37 9 F6
Peter James Cl TN31 18 B5
Peter James La TN35 12 B2
Pett Level Rd,
Hastings TN35 12 D4
Pett Level Rd,
Winchelsea TN36 19 C6
Pett Rd TN35 11 H4
Pevensey Rd TN34 15 F4
Philip Cole Cl TN34 3 F2
Picardy Cl TN33 4 D3
Pilgrims Way TN34 10 B6
Pilot Rd TN34 3 B3
Piltdown Cl, Bexhill TN39 6 C4
Piltdown Cl,
Hastings TN34 16 A4
Pinders Rd TN35 17 E3
Pinders Walk TN35 17 F2
Pine Av TN34 16 D1
Pinewood Way TN38 8 C6
Pinewoods TN39 6 C3
Pipers Cl TN40 6 D2
Playden Gdns TN34 10 D6
Plemont Gdns TN39 6 B3
Plough La TN37 9 F3
Plover Ct TN38 8 C6
Plumpton Cl TN40 6 D2
Plynlimmon Rd TN34 3 E2
Point Hill TN31 20 D2
Polegrove Pk TN39 6 B6
Ponswood Ind Est
TN38 15 F1
Ponswood Rd TN38 15 F1
Poppa La TN38 5 B5
Port St TN34 3 D2
Portfield Cl TN40 7 E3
Portland Pl TN34 3 F2
Post Office Pass TN34 3 F2
Post Office Pass*,
High St TN34 16 C5
Pottingfield Rd TN31 20 A3
Powdermill La TN33 4 D4
Preston Rd TN39 6 C1
Primrose Hill,
Bexhill TN39 6 A3
Primrose Hill,
Hastings TN35 13 E4
Princes Rd TN37 15 H4
Priory Av TN34 3 A1
Priory Cl TN34 3 B1
Priory Mdw
Shopping Centre TN34 3 C2
Priory Rd TN34 3 A1
Priory St TN34 3 C3
Priory Ter TN34 16 B3
Prospect Pl TN34 3 B3
Providence Way TN34 9 G3
Prowting Mead TN39 6 B1
Putlands Cres TN39 6 B1

Quantock Gdns TN34 16 D1
Quarry Cres TN34 16 C3
Quarry Hill TN38 15 F4
Quarry Ho TN35 15 F5
Quarry Rd TN34 16 B3
Quarry Ter TN34 16 B3
Quebec Cl TN39 9 E6
Quebec Rd TN34 3 D1
Queens Rd TN34 3 C2
Queens Sq TN34 3 C2
Queensway TN38 8 B6

Radcliffe Cl TN37 9 G5
Radnor Mews TN38 14 D1
Railway Cotts TN38 14 D5
Ranmore Cl TN34 10 A5
Raven Ct, Battle TN33 4 E3
Raven Ct,
St Leonards TN38 8 C6
Ravens Cl TN38 5 B5
Ravenside Retail
& Leisure Pk TN40 7 G4
Ravine Cl TN34 16 C2
Rayford Ct TN40 6 D4
Rectory Rd TN38 15 F2
Rectory La, TN34 20 C1
Rectory La,
Winchelsea TN36 19 A3
Rectory Way TN40 7 E3
Red Barn Mews TN33 4 D3
Red Lake Ter TN35 17 F1
Redgeland Rise TN38 14 D1
Redmayne Dr TN34 3 A3
Reedswood Rd TN38 14 C3
Regency Gdns TN38 15 E3
Regent Pl TN37 8 D2
Regent Sq TN31 20 C3
Reginald Rd TN39 6 C5
Renown Cl TN40 7 E2
Reynolds Dr TN40 7 E3
Richborough Cl TN34 9 H5
Richland Cl TN35 17 F1
Richmond Av TN38 9 A6
Richmond Cl TN39 6 B6
Richmond Gro TN39 6 A6
Richmond Rd TN34 16 B3
Richmond St TN34 16 D3
Riders Bolt TN39 5 D3
Ridge West Ind Est
TN37 9 F2
Ridgewood Gdns,
Bexhill TN40 7 F4
Ridgewood Gdns,
Hastings TN34 10 A5
Ringwood Mews TN38 14 D1
Ringwood Rd TN38 14 D1
Robert Tressell Cl TN34 16 A3
Roberts Hill TN36 19 A2
Robertson Pass TN34 3 C3
Robertson Pass*,
Robertson St TN34 16 A5
Robertson St TN34 3 B3
Robertsons Hill TN34 16 D3
Robin Hill TN39 5 C4
Robsack Av TN38 14 C1
Rochester Rd TN37 15 G1
Rock Channel East TN31 20 D3
Rock Channel Quay TN31 20 D3
Rock Cl TN35 11 E6
Rock La TN35 11 E2
Rock-a-Nore Rd TN34 3 F3
Rocklands La TN35 17 E4
Rockmead Rd TN35 13 E5
Roebuck St TN34 3 F2
Roedean Cl TN39 5 C5
Rookery La TN36 19 B2
Rookhurst Rd TN40 7 G4
Roosevelt Ct TN38 9 F6
Rope Walk TN31 20 C3
Rope Walk Arc TN31 20 C3
Roselands Rd TN34 6 A3
Rosemary La TN31 12 B2
Rother Ct TN39 5 B5
Rotherfield Av,
Bexhill TN40 7 E4
Rotherfield Av,
Hastings TN34 16 D3
Rothsay Rd TN38 15 G4
Roundacres Way TN40 7 F3
Roundwood Rd TN37 9 F4
Rowan Cl TN38 9 H3
Rowan Gdns TN40 7 F3
Rowbarns TN33 4 C1
Royal Military Rd TN36 19 B2
Royston Gdns TN40 7 F3
Rue De Bayeux TN33 4 D3
Rushmere Rise TN38 14 C2
Russell Ct TN34 3 E3
Russell Ct*,
George St TN34 16 C5
Russell St TN34 3 D3
Rye Hill TN31 20 C2
Rye Ind Pk TN31 20 D3
Rye Rd TN35 11 F6
Rymill Rd TN38 9 F6

Sackville Rd TN39 6 C5
St Andrews Rd TN40 6 C5
St Andrews Sq TN34 3 D2
St Annes Cl TN40 7 E3
St Augustines Cl TN39 6 B4
St Catherines Cl TN37 15 H3
St Davids Av TN40 6 D4
St Dominic Cl TN34 15 E4
St Francis Chase TN39 6 B3
St Georges Rd,
Bexhill TN40 6 C3
St Georges Rd,
Hastings TN34 16 C3
St Giles Cl TN36 19 A3
St Helens Av TN34 16 A1
St Helens Cres TN34 16 A3
St Helens Ct TN34 16 A3
St Helens Park Rd,
Blacklands TN34 16 A3
St Helens Park Rd,
St Helens TN34 10 B5
St Helens Rd TN34 9 G5
St Helens Wood Rd TN34 10 A6
St James Av TN40 6 D2
St James Cl TN40 6 D2
St James Cres TN40 6 D2
St James Rd, Bexhill TN40 6 D2
St James Rd,
Hastings TN34 16 B4
St Johns Rd, Bexhill TN40 6 D3
St Johns Rd,
St Leonards TN37 15 G4
St Lawrence Rd TN34 6 C2
St Leonards Ct TN38 15 E5
St Leonards Rd TN40 6 D5
St Margarets Rd TN34 3 A4
St Margarets Ter,
Rye TN31 20 C4
St Margarets Ter,
St Leonards TN37 15 H4
St Marks Cl TN39 5 C3
St Marys La TN39 6 A1
St Marys Rd TN34 3 A3
St Marys Ter, Battle TN33 4 E4
St Marys Ter,
Hastings TN34 3 E1
St Marys Villas TN33 9 E3
St Matthews Dr TN38 15 G2
St Matthews Gdns TN38 15 F2
St Matthews Rd TN38 15 F2
St Patricks Cres TN40 6 D3
St Pauls Cl TN37 15 H4
St Pauls Pl TN37 15 H4
St Pauls Rd TN37 15 G3
St Peters Cres TN40 7 E3
St Peters Ct TN40 7 E4
St Peters Rd TN37 15 G2
St Saviours Rd TN38 15 H2
St Thomas St TN36 19 B2
St Thomass s Rd TN34 16 C4
St Vincents Rd TN38 14 D4
Salcey Cl TN35 14 C1
Salehurst Gdns TN38 14 C1
Salisbury Rd,
Bexhill TN40 6 C4
Salisbury Rd,
St Leonards TN35 15 G2
Saltcote La TN31 20 C1
Saltdean Cl TN39 5 D5
Saltdean Way TN39 5 C5
Salters La TN34 3 F1
Salvington Cres TN39 6 A4
San Jose Cl TN35 17 E3
Sandhurst Gdns TN40 10 B5
Sandhurst La TN35 5 A3
Sandown Rd TN35 17 E2
Sandown Way TN40 7 F3
Sandringham Heights
TN38 8 B6
Sandrock Hill TN36 19 A3
Sandrock Pk TN40 10 B5
Sandwich Dr TN38 15 E3
Sandy Cl TN37 9 F4
Saunders Cl TN34 16 B3
Saunders Way TN31 18 C6
Saxby Rd TN39 5 C3
Saxon Ct TN37 15 G3
Saxon Rd TN35 17 F2
Saxon Rise TN40 7 F4
Saxon St TN37 15 G5
Saxonhurst Cl TN37 9 F5
Saxonwood Rd TN37 4 C3
School Cl TN31 20 B3
School Hill TN34 19 A2
School Pl TN40 7 G4
School Rd TN35 17 E2
Schwerte Way TN34 3 A4
Scotts Acre TN31 18 B5
Scutes Cl TN34 16 B2
Sea Rd, Bexhill TN40 6 D6
Sea Rd, Hastings TN35 13 F5
Sea Rd, Rye TN31 18 B6
Sea Rd,
St Leonards TN38 14 D5
Sea Rd,
Winchelsea TN36 19 B2
Seabourne Rd TN40 7 F2
Seaside Pass TN38 14 D5
Seaside Rd TN38 14 D5
Seaview Ter TN36 19 B2
Second Av, Bexhill TN40 7 G3
Second Av, Rye TN31 18 B6
Sedgebrook Gdns TN35 15 H1
Sedgewick Rd TN40 7 F3
Sedlescombe Gdns TN38 15 F1
Sedlescombe Rd North
TN37 9 F3
Sedlescombe Rd South
TN38 15 F2
Selmeston Cl TN34 15 H2
Senlac Cl TN33 4 C2
Senlac Gdns TN33 4 E4
Senlac Way TN37 9 G4
Seven Acre Cl TN37 9 E3
Sewell Av TN40 6 C3
Seymour Villas TN34 16 B2
Sheerwater Cres TN34 9 H5
Shepherd St*,
Shepherd St TN38 15 G5
Shepherd St TN38 15 G5
Shepherds Cl TN39 5 C4
Shepherds Cl TN35 12 D5
Shepherds Way TN35 13 E5

23

Name	Ref
Sheppard Pl TN33	4 C2
Sherwood Cl TN34	16 B3
Shingle Ct TN38	8 C2
Shining Cliff TN35	10 B6
Shipley La TN39	5 C5
Shipyard La TN31	20 C4
Shirlea Vw TN33	4 D3
Shirley Dr TN37	9 F5
Sidley Grn TN39	6 C2
Sidley St TN39	6 C1
Sidney Little Rd TN38	8 C6
Silchester Rd TN38	15 G4
Silva Cl TN40	7 G2
Silvan Rd TN38	8 D5
Silverhill Av TN37	9 G5
Silverlands Rd TN37	15 F1
Silvester Rd TN40	7 H3
Singleton Walk TN40	7 H3
Sinnock Sq TN34	3 F2
Sinnock Sq*, High St TN34	16 C5
Smeatons La TN36	19 D4
Smithys Cl TN37	9 G4
Smugglers Way TN35	13 E5
South Cliff TN39	5 D5
South Cliff Av TN39	5 D5
South St TN37	9 G4
South Ter, Hastings TN34	3 C2
South Ter, Westfield TN35	10 C2
South Undercliff TN31	20 C4
Southcourt Av TN34	6 A6
Southdown Av TN34	16 D2
Southlands Av TN39	6 B1
Southlands Rd TN39	6 B1
Southport Cl TN38	15 E4
Southwater Rd TN37	15 G3
Southwood Cl TN38	15 F2
Sovereign Cl TN40	10 C6
Sovereign Mews TN38	15 E5
Spindlewood Dr TN39	5 B4
Sprays La TN33	10 A1
Spring La TN39	5 B3
Spring Steps TN36	19 B2
Springfield Ct TN31	20 B1
Springfield Rd, Bexhill TN40	6 C3
Springfield Rd, St Leonards TN38	15 F2
Springfield Valley Rd TN38	15 F2
Springside Walk TN38	14 D2
Squirrel Cl, Bexhill TN39	5 D2
Squirrel Cl, St Leonards TN38	8 D6
Stable Mews TN37	9 G4
Stablefield TN35	10 C2
Stainsby St TN37	15 G4
Stamford Ct TN35	17 E3
Stanhope Pl TN38	15 G5
Stanier Rd TN38	8 D4
Stanley Rd TN38	3 B2
Starrs Green La TN33	4 F4
Starrs Grn TN33	4 E4
Starrs Mead TN33	4 F4
Starwell Cl TN38	9 H6
Station App, Battle TN33	4 E4
Station App, Hastings TN34	3 C2
Station App, Rye TN31	20 C3
Station App, St Leonards TN37	15 G4
Station Rd, Bexhill TN40	6 C3
Station Rd, Hastings TN34	3 C3
Station Rd, Winchelsea TN36	19 A1
Stevens Cl TN39	6 D2
Stirling Rd TN38	9 E4
Stock Dale TN35	13 E5
Stockleigh Rd TN38	3 D2
Stone St TN34	3 D2
Stonebeach Rise TN38	8 C2
Stonefield Rd TN34	3 D1
Stonefield Rd TN34	3 D2
Stonehouse Dr TN38	15 E1
Stonelink Cl TN37	8 D2
Stonestile La, St Helens TN35	10 B4
Stonestile La, Westfield TN35	10 B4
Strand TN31	20 C3
Strand Hill TN36	19 B2
Stream La TN35	13 F4
Streamside Cl TN34	16 A2
Strome Ho TN33	6 D2
Strongs Pass*, All Saints St TN34	16 D5
Strood Rd TN37	15 G1
Sturdee Pl TN34	3 E3
Suffolk Rd TN39	6 C2
Summer Hill TN38	15 E3
Summer Hill Rd TN39	6 A3
Sunningdale Cl TN40	7 E4
Sunningdale Dr TN38	14 D4
Sussex Cl TN39	6 A4
Sussex Rd TN38	15 E5
Sutherland Av TN39	6 B4
Sutherland Cl TN39	6 A4
Sutton TN40	7 F5
Suttons Ind Pk TN36	19 C2
Swaines Pass*, All Saints St TN34	16 D5
Swallow Bank TN38	14 D1
Swallow Dr TN33	4 F3
Swan Ter TN34	3 F2
Swynford Dr TN38	9 E4
Sycamore Cl, Bexhill TN39	5 B3
Sycamore Cl, St Leonards TN38	15 E2
Sydney Cl TN38	9 F6
Tackleway TN34	16 D5
Tall Ash Cl TN34	9 G5
Tanglewood Coppice TN39	5 D4
Tangmere Cl TN39	5 D5
Tanyard Cotts TN36	19 B2
Tanyard La TN36	19 A2
Taylor Cl TN38	8 D5
Teal Ct TN38	8 C5
Tedder Ter TN35	11 E6
Telford Rd TN38	9 E4
Telham TN34	10 C6
Tenterden Rise TN34	16 A2
Terminus Av TN39	6 B5
Terminus Rd TN39	6 B5
Terrace Rd TN37	15 G4
Testers Cotts TN35	17 F1
Thakeham Cl TN40	7 G3
Thanet Way TN34	16 A3
The Avenue TN35	13 E5
The Barnhams TN39	5 D5
The Beeches TN38	8 D3
The Bourne TN34	3 F3
The Briary TN40	7 E3
The Broadwalk TN35	5 A3
The Broadway TN35	17 F1
The Byeway, Bexhill TN39	5 C3
The Byeway, Hastings TN34	16 B1
The Cheviots TN34	16 D1
The Cloisters, Battle TN33	4 C1
The Cloisters, St Leonards TN37	15 H4
The Close, Hastings TN35	12 B6
The Close, Rye TN31	20 B2
The Coppice, Battle TN33	4 F4
The Coppice, Hastings TN34	3 B1
The Courtyard TN34	3 A1
The Covert TN39	5 B5
The Crescent TN34	9 G6
The Croft TN34	3 F2
The Deals*, The Quay TN31	20 C3
The Dene TN35	10 C5
The Drive TN38	15 E3
The Fairway, Bexhill TN39	6 A2
The Fairway, St Leonards TN38	14 D3
The Finches, Bexhill TN40	7 F4
The Finches, St Leonards TN38	9 E4
The Gables TN34	16 A1
The Glades, Bexhill TN40	7 E3
The Glades, St Leonards TN37	9 E4
The Glebe, Hastings TN34	16 C3
The Glebe, Pett TN35	13 E1
The Gorses TN39	5 B6
The Gorseway TN39	5 B3
The Green, Rye TN31	20 C4
The Green, St Leonards TN38	15 F2
The Grove, Battle TN33	4 F4
The Grove, Bexhill TN39	5 D3
The Grove, Rye TN31	20 C2
The Hawthorns TN37	8 D2
The Heights TN35	17 G1
The Highlands TN37	6 A1
The Hoe TN37	9 F3
The Kestrels TN38	9 E4
The Lawn TN35	15 G4
The Link TN31	20 A3
The Links TN38	14 D3
The Mead TN39	5 C4
The Meadows TN37	9 G4
The Mint TN31	20 C3
The Mount TN35	15 F4
The Oak Fld TN35	13 E1
The Oakfield TN31	20 C1
The Oaks TN37	9 H3
The Quay TN31	20 B3
The Ridge, Hastings TN34	9 H3
The Ridge, St Leonards TN37	9 F2
The Ridge, Winchelsea TN36	19 D5
The Ridge West TN37	8 D2
The Ridings, Bexhill TN39	6 A1
The Ridings, St Leonards TN38	9 G4
The Roundel TN37	9 H4
The Sedges TN38	14 C2
The Shrublands TN39	5 D5
The Slides TN38	9 E6
The Spaldings TN38	14 D2
The Spinney, Battle TN33	4 F4
The Spinney, Bexhill TN39	5 D5
The Spinney, Hastings TN34	16 A4
The Suttons, Rye TN31	18 C6
The Suttons, St Leonards TN38	14 A4
The Thorns TN35	11 H3
The Twitten TN39	5 C3
The Uplands TN38	15 F4
The Woodlands TN34	10 A5
The Yeaklen Dr TN38	15 F1
Third Av TN40	7 G3
Thomas Brassey Cl TN37	9 F4
Thornbank Cres TN39	6 A5
Ticehurst Cl TN35	16 D1
Tile Barn Rd TN38	8 D5
Tilekiln La TN35	17 G1
Tilgate Dr TN39	5 C5
Tillingham Av TN31	20 B3
Tillington Ter*, Ashburnham Rd TN35	16 D3
Tithe Barn Fld TN36	18 C2
Tiverton Dr TN40	7 F4
Tollgates TN33	4 A3
Tonbridge Way TN31	18 B5
Top Cross Rd TN40	7 G2
Torfield TN34	16 D4
Tower Rd TN37	15 G2
Tower Rd West TN38	15 F3
Tower St TN31	20 C3
Towerscroft Av TN37	9 F4
Town Hall Sq TN34	6 C5
Trafalgar Cl TN37	8 D2
Travellers La TN35	17 E1
Trinity St TN34	3 B3
Trinity St*, Robertson St TN34	16 A5
Trinity Villas TN34	3 B3
Trinity Villas*, White Rock Rd TN34	16 A6
Truman Dr TN38	8 D2
Tudor Av TN38	15 E4
Tudor Ct TN39	6 A5
Tuppenney Cl TN35	16 D1
Turkey Rd TN39	5 C1
Turkeycock La*, Conduit Hill TN31	20 C3
Turnberry Cl TN38	14 D4
Turner Cl TN40	7 E3
Twyford Cres TN37	9 G5
Tyndale Av TN39	5 B4
Uckham La TN33	4 D1
Udimore Rd TN31	20 A4
Undercliff TN38	15 F5
Union St TN38	15 G4
Uplands Cl TN39	6 A2
Upper Broomgrove Rd TN34	16 C2
Upper Church Rd TN37	9 F5
Upper Clarence Rd TN37	15 G1
Upper Glen Rd TN37	9 E4
Upper Lake TN33	4 D3
Upper Maze Hill TN38	15 F3
Upper Park TN37	15 G2
Upper Sea Rd TN40	6 D5
Upper South Rd TN37	15 G2
Vale Rd, Battle TN33	4 A3
Vale Rd, St Leonards TN37	15 G1
Valleyside Rd TN35	16 D2
Vantage Walk TN38	15 F4
Venture Cl TN40	7 F4
Vermont Way TN38	8 D3
Vicarage La TN35	10 B2
Vicarage Rd TN35	10 B2
Victoria Av TN35	17 E1
Victoria Cl TN38	15 F5
Victoria Rd, Bexhill TN39	6 C5
Victoria Rd, St Leonards TN37	15 H4
Victoria Way TN36	19 D5
View Bank TN35	17 F2
Villa Rd TN37	15 H4
Village Cl TN39	5 B3
Village Mews TN39	5 B4
Vinehall Cl TN34	10 B6
Virgins Cft TN33	4 D1
Virgins La TN33	4 C1
Wadhurst Cl TN37	9 F4
Wainwright Cl TN38	8 B6
Wainwright Rd TN38	6 C5
Waites La TN35	12 D4
Wakehams Cl TN39	6 C2
Waldegrave St TN34	3 D2
Waldene Cl TN34	16 B2
Waldon Ter TN33	4 D3
Walton Cl TN37	9 G4
Walton Pk TN39	6 A5
Wannock Cl TN40	7 G3
Ward Way TN39	6 A3
Warnham Gdns TN40	7 E2
Warren Cl TN38	14 C3
Warren Rd TN35	12 B6
Warrior Gdns TN37	15 G4
Warrior Sq TN37	15 G4
Wartling Cl TN38	8 D6
Warwick Rd TN39	6 A4
Washington Av TN38	8 D3
Watchbell La TN31	20 C3
Watchbell St TN31	20 C4
Water Mint Cl TN38	14 C2
Watergate TN39	6 C1
Waterloo Cl TN37	9 E2
Waterloo Pl*, The Bourne TN34	16 D5
Watermens Cl TN34	16 A2
Watermill Cl TN39	6 C1
Watermill Dr TN38	8 B6
Watermill La, Bexhill TN39	6 C5
Watermill La, Guestling Green TN35	12 B1
Watermill La, Icklesham TN35,36	18 A3
Waterside Cl TN35	16 D2
Watersmeet Cotts TN34	3 D1
Waterworks Rd TN34	3 D1
Wattles Wish TN33	4 C1
Wealden Way TN39	5 B2
Welbeck Av TN38	15 E5
Wellesley Cl TN39	5 C5
Wellesley TN34	3 F2
Wellington Gdns TN33	4 C2
Wellington Mews TN34	3 D2
Wellington Pl TN34	3 C3
Wellington Rd TN34	3 D2
Wellington Sq TN34	3 D3
Wellis Gdns TN35	15 E3
Wellplace Cotts TN36	18 D2
Wentworth Cl TN40	7 F4
Wentworth Way TN38	14 D3
West Ascent TN38	15 F5
West Down Rd TN39	6 B4
West Hill Mews TN34	14 D5
West Hill Rd TN34	14 D5
West Marina TN38	14 D5
West Par TN39	6 B6
West St, Hastings TN34	3 E3
West St, Rye TN31	20 C3
West Undercliff TN34	20 A4
West Vw TN34	16 D3
Westaway Dr TN39	6 B5
Westbourne Cl TN39	5 B6
Westbrook La TN35	10 C1
Westdean Cl TN37	9 G3
Westerleigh Cl TN38	15 E3
Western Av TN33	4 C3
Western Rd, Bexhill TN40	6 C5
Western Rd, St Leonards TN37	15 G4
Westfield La, Hastings TN35	10 C3
Westfield La, St Leonards TN38	9 F2
Westham Cl TN39	5 D5
Westminster Cres TN34	16 C1
Westville Rd TN39	6 B5
Whatlington Rd TN33	4 D1
Whatlington Way TN38	14 C1
Wheatfield Cl TN37	9 G4
Wheel Farm Bsns Pk TN35	10 B2
Wheel La TN35	10 A1
White Hill Av TN39	5 D3
White Hill Dr TN39	5 D4
White Rock TN37	3 A4
White Rock Gdns TN34	3 B4
White Rock Rd TN34	3 A4
Whitefriars Rd TN34	16 C4
Whitehouse Av TN39	6 B2
Whittingtons Way TN34	16 C1
Whittlewood Cl TN38	14 D1
Whitworth Rd TN37	9 F2
Whydown Rd TN39	5 B1
Wickham Av TN39	6 B6
Wickham Rock Rd TN36	19 A4
Wilkins Way TN40	7 G2
William Rd TN38	14 C4
Willingdon Av, Bexhill TN39	6 B4
Willingdon Av, St Leonards TN38	9 E4
Willingdon Cl TN38	9 E4
Willingdon Way TN38	9 E4
Willow Dr TN39	5 B3
Willow End TN34	16 B1
Willow La TN36	19 D4
Willowbed Walk TN34	10 A6
Wilmington Rd TN34	16 D3
Wilton Rd TN40	6 D6
Winceby Cl TN38	5 D6
Winchelsea La TN35	11 F5
Winchelsea Rd, Hastings TN35	17 E1
Winchelsea Rd, Rye TN31	20 B4
Windgrove Cotts TN33	4 D1
Windgrove Ho TN33	4 D1
Winding Dr TN34	3 F3
Winding St*, The Bourne TN34	16 C5
Windmill Cl TN36	19 C3
Windmill Dr TN39	6 B2
Windmill Rd TN38	15 F1
Windmill Way TN36	19 B3
Windsor Rd, Bexhill TN39	6 C5
Windsor Rd, St Leonards TN37	9 F6
Windsor Way TN36	19 C5
Wineham Way TN40	7 F4
Wingate Cl TN38	15 E2
Winston Dr TN39	5 D4
Winterbourne Cl TN34	3 A2
Wish St TN31	20 C3
Wish Ward TN31	20 C3
Wishing Tree Cl TN38	14 D1
Wishing Tree Rd TN38	14 D1
Wishing Tree Rd North TN38	9 E5
Withyham Rd TN39	5 B5
Woodbrook Rd TN34	16 B2
Woodcombe TN34	16 A1
Woodhams Cl TN33	4 C3
Woodland Rise TN34	7 G4
Woodland Vale Rd TN37	15 G3
Woodland Way TN35	12 D5
Woodlands Way TN34	10 A5
Woods Pass*, All Saints St TN34	16 D5
Woodsgate Av TN40	6 C3
Woodsgate Pk TN39	6 B3
Woodspring Cl TN37	9 G3
Woodstock Rd TN39	5 B2
Woodville Rd TN39	6 B4
Workhouse La, Hastings TN35	10 C2
Workhouse La, Winchelsea TN36	18 D2
Worsham La TN39	7 F1
Wren Ct, Battle TN33	4 F3
Wren Ct, St Leonards TN38	8 C6
Wrestwood Cl TN40	6 D2
Wrestwood Rd TN40	6 D2
Wrotham Cl TN34	10 A5
Wychurst Gdns TN40	7 E3
Wykeham Rd TN34	3 A1
Yates Cl TN31	18 C6
Yew Tree Cl TN34	10 A5
York Gdns TN34	3 C3
York Rd, Bexhill TN40	7 H3
York Rd, St Leonards TN37	15 G1